D1092795

Roundabouts
From The Air *ish*

Roundabouts From The Air *ish*

Kevin Beresford

NEW HOLLAND

Introduction

"I am a rock, I am an island," Paul Simon.

I wish I had a pound for every time a roundabout enthusiast has said to me "I thought I was the only one who loved those things." The success of my *Roundabouts of Great Britain* book has dragged a huge amount of roundabout spotters out of the closet and granted them the confidence to stand up and say "I love roundabouts and I'm proud!".

A very emotional long distance truck driver telephoned last year to say that he'd heard my interview that morning on BBC Radio Scotland and was overjoyed to learn for the first time in his life that someone else shared the same flaming passion for roundabout spotting. After listening with growing excitement to the radio broadcast he explained to me he'd got so agitated he had to pull over at the nearest lay-by to call and thank me.

Apparently my well-wisher had been a dedicated roundabout spotter for years, not just in Britain but also on the Continent (mainly France), collecting over time, a hugely diverse range of photographs and data on traffic islands and gyratory systems.

Amazingly, he had kept his hobby a secret from his wife and friends, for fear of ridicule. Upon discovering that there is a growing body of roundabout enthusiasts out there, he felt he could now bring his secret out in the open and practise his passion in public and even tell the wife. Praise the 'bout!

Roundabouts of Great Britain has also converted new disciples to the cause. After reading the book, people who otherwise had not given traffic islands a second glance now gaze upon them with awe and respect.

God's Wonderful Roundabouts, they've always been with us, right in front of our eyes, every day of the year. Now they are finally being viewed and appreciated in a new light. Roads are often condemned as being scars on the landscape but with the coming of roundabouts in all their glory, they counteract the road's unsightliness. With infinite variety, colour and creative-ness, these bitumen beauties lift our sagging spirits on long tiresome trips. On road systems anywhere in the world there is nothing more expressive than the roundabout. The roundabout is truly an oasis on a sea of asphalt.

Enough waxing lyrical, I must now hold my hands up and admit to some glaring omissions in the last roundabout book, mainly Scotland and a good chunk of South East England, including London would you believe. Following hundreds of irate calls and e-mails I'm pleased to announce that these areas are now included. In fact my venture north of the border unearthed some real gyratory gems. The Scots really know how to build roundabouts. Livingston, I presume, must be really proud of their brilliant brick 'bouts.

I've also tried to cover more of the larger 'bouts, by introducing aerial shots. This has included taking a few risks on the top of tall office buildings, greasing the palms of caretakers in penthouse apartments, standing on mates shoulders and scampering up a few trees and hills, just to capture the roundabout in perspective with its surroundings. The more unusual roundabouts of Britain have also been sought out and captured.

So join me on a journey across the Happy Roundabout Hunting Grounds of Milton Keynes. Let's leave our footprints in the sand and traffic-island hop along the shimmering shores of Blackpool. Come fly with me across the fertile roundabout plains of Norwich. Experience the Magic Rings of Swindon. Discover the intoxicating aromas of a Grimsby fishing 'bout. Allow me to be your guide and drive you around the bend, around the roundabouts of Britain.

Kevin Beresford
Lord of the Rings
President of U.K.R.A.S.

USEFUL ROUNDABOUT JARGON

BONKING BOUTERS – *see page 116.*

'BOUTS – *abbreviation of roundabouts.*

BRICKIE – *a roundabout consisting of bricks only.*

CHEVY – *a roundabout with inclined chevron brick work.*

CRUSOE – *an extremely large and lush island, mainly uninhabited.*

DESERT ISLAND – *a boring island with nothing on it.*

DOUBLE RINGER – *an island made up of a raised inner core and a lower outer core.*

GEEK ISLANDER – *A roundabout spotter who takes our hobby too seriously.*

GREEK ISLAND – *a roundabout that boasts a statue, sculpture or monument etc.*

G.W.R. – *God's Wonderful Roundabouts.*

KNIGHT OF THE ROUNDABOUT TABLE – *fully fledged, signed-up, initiated, paid up, has a funny handshake, card carrying member of the UK Roundabout Appreciation Society. Damsels welcome.*

KNIGHT OF THE INNER RING – *fully fledged, signed-up, initiated, paid up, has a funny handshake, card carrying member of the UK Roundabout Appreciation Society, (but with duties). Damsels welcome.*

LORD OF THE RINGS – *President of U.K.R.A.S.*

P.M.T. – *Painted Mini Traffic island.*

RED RINGER – *a roundabout with a red painted ring around its perimeter (not an ailment).*

RING MASTER – *Chairman, U.K.R.A.S.*

ROUNDABOUT RING – *A group of like-minded roundabout spotters who have formed their own club. Perfectly respectable and legal.*

ROUNDABOUT SPOTTER – *a dedicated traffic island enthusiast, always wears a cheerful smile no matter what the weather. Turns the other cheek in the face of ridicule. Is never without his/her thermos flask and anorak.*

SPECTACULAR! SPECTACULAR! – *roundabout with a WOW! factor.*

TOKER – *grass only roundabout.*

TITCHMARSH TRAFFIC ISLAND – *a roundabout with flowers in full bloom.*

U.K.R.A.S. – *acronym, the United Kingdom Roundabout Appreciation Society.*

A brilliant Bracknell "Crusoe" roundabout, looking very lush and green.

Subways on roundabouts these days are out of fashion with local councils due to muggings etc. However, the walkway on this island looks very enticing indeed, like a stroll in an English country garden, so to speak. Just don't forget the mace spray after dark.

A Worcester roundabout comprised of flags, flowers, lawn, trees and rather tall curved kerbstones. Worcester Cathedral is just a few yards away, out of shot.

This terrific "Titchmarsh" traffic-island was spotted on the London Road, Nottingham. A beautiful display of lawn, flowers and trees. A delightful walkway has been provided by Nottingham Council.

How lovely to be tied up in Notts for an hour or two to soak up the atmosphere of this island. The BBC studios can be seen in the background.

Pagoda roundabout, Holloway Circus, Birmingham City Centre.

An amazing aerial shot of this roundabout undergoing a bit of a make-over.

The close-up photograph depicts an authentic pagoda, handcrafted in the Fujian province of China. This pagoda was a gift to the people of Birmingham from local businessman Wing Yip.

Special thanks must go to construction worker David Pollock who scaled the heights of one of Brum's tallest buildings to capture this moment – a rebirth of a roundabout... AWESOME!

Smashing elevated shot of a Merry Hill, Black Country roundabout. This delightful island is comprised of coloured gravel, shrubs, bushes and trees. Note the old clock keeping watch behind the bushes.

A jolly juxtaposition of flowers and shrubs encompassed by bright brickwork.

It won't be long before they introduce garden decking. A true "Titchmarsh". This beautiful arrangement was spotted in Norwich.

Brian's birthday 'bout based in Airdrie.

Couldn't they have chosen a more colourful roundabout to celebrate his birthday?

Terrific observation of the Eastern Daily Press roundabout, captured on a beautiful spring day. Another Norwich "Spectacular! Spectacular!"

Brilliant bird's eye view of Lambeth Palace roundabout featuring an arty arrangement of brick and tall slender trees. The shot was taken from a TV personality's penthouse apartment rooftop. (It's a long story.)

The famous Whirlies roundabout from East Kilbride.

Note those wonderful whirly metal ball sculptures. The whole scene seems to be in a bit of a whirl.

Delightful patterned "brickie" spotted in Plymouth. The brickwork actually matches the colour of the local buses.

Its crowning glory is a fine ornate double lamppost. 10 out of 10 goes to Plymouth for the analogous harmony.

Grimy "chevy" gyratory called Canal Circle in Manchester. It's ironic that the world's first roundabouts in America were called "circles" and people in Manchester call their roundabouts "circles". Why is that?

Atmospheric, dusky, autumnal Milton Keynes roundabout made up of bushes and trees with an outer brick ring. If Monet were alive he would be painting roundabouts.

The Bubbles roundabout, Livingston, Scotland.

A plain brickie with a few directional signs and one solitary lamppost. It doesn't look that bubbly to me.

Topiary-inspired traffic island set inside a Black Country retail park. A superb combination of "chevy" brickwork and sculptured trees and bushes, this 'bout represents British roundabout craftsmanship at its best. Quite remarkable.

"The Bowling Green" pub, Lichfield. To my knowledge one of only two public houses in Great Britain that are built on roundabouts, the other being "The Shepherd & Flock" Farnham, Surrey.

Elevated shot of a "toker" traffic island, spotted in the West Midlands.

For those who are interested in these things, the shot was taken from the top rung of a rusty fire escape on a nearby factory.

Mysterious Airdrie spiral brick 'bout topped with stainless steel tubes.

What does it all mean?

EXTREME ROUNDABOUTING

I've recently exchanged correspondence with the Features Editor of "Fast Bikes" magazine, Jamie Wilkins. Jamie has informed me of a growing craze amongst motor bikers labelled "Roundabout Surfing". The practice consists of lapping a roundabout at speed with your knee and elbow touching the surface of the road... while you are on your bike of course. The roundabout apparently needs to be of a decent size, with a grippy and smooth surface and a minimum of traffic and exits.

Now, I have to say Jamie is an avid fan of roundabouts but I was slightly alarmed at the prospect of this trend catching on. I tabled my concerns to the bi-monthly meeting of the UK Roundabout Appreciation Society, who shared my worry. After much deliberation and debate the following statement from U.K.R.A.S. was released:

"We the committee cannot endorse this extreme, and to our minds, reckless act of so called 'Roundabout Surfing'. It comes across to us as a dangerous and noisy pursuit. As a committee however, on reflection, we don't want to appear killjoys when it comes to people's enjoyment. We suggest, as a compromise, why not carry on surfing on your motorbike but with a sidecar attached and only at a steady 15 m.p.h.? Make sure you are going slowly so that there is no danger of your sidecar lifting off the ground. We are sure all you bikers out there will heartily agree to this request."

Alvechurch Roundabout Surfers Club with team leader Max Handford on bike 57, enjoying the ultimate surf at Oulstone Park Roundabout.
His sister Joanne is on bike 56.

Hang on guys, where are the sidecars?

Further proof of roundabouts' infinite variety.

Set on a quaint cobbled Bath square this 'bout features a towering old tree encompassed by paving slabs and strange stone bollards.

To the right of the tree stands my seven-year-old son Ben who is clearly following in his father's footsteps, in his own love of roundabouts.

You can always rely on a M.K. roundabout. Their perfect symmetry, the well-kept lawns, tasteful trees. An M.K. 'bout will never let you down. Viewed from a Milton Keynes flyover.

Another Coventry "cutie". This one's a double ringer.

Its inner core is made up of grass and the outer ring is composed of brickwork. In the summer months the lamppost in the middle is draped with gorgeous hanging baskets bursting with blooms. However, this picture was taken in January.

A riveting Redditch "Crusoe".

The picture was taken from one of the many Redditch concrete bridges that spans one of the many concrete dual carriageways that cover Redditch.

The Globe gyratory in Alcester. Very neat and tidy 'bout. The globe structure in the centre of the island promotes peace and goodwill. A great combination of metal sculpture, grass, flowers, brickwork and a sense of well-being.

Scintillating view of a well designed P.M.T. "red ringer" spotted in the village of Barnt Green.
The photograph was taken from the local railway embankment.

Bone island in Skelmersdale.
A fine example of an isthmus
joining two large islands.

ARE WE FINALLY READY TO EMBRACE THE ROAD?

For the first time ever a road was voted Britain's best public "building" in 2004. The road in question was the A650 Bingley Relief Road. Its 3-mile journey takes it through the Yorkshire town of Bingley, over a railway, three bogs, a canal and a contaminated waste site.

The £45.5m road was up against stiff competition from a Scottish viaduct, the revamped Trafalgar Square and a state-of-the-art public lavatory in Hampshire.

The body granting this award was C.A.B.E. – The Commission for Architecture and the Built Environment. This building award tends to be given to well…buildings, but finally, slowly but surely, people everywhere are waking up to the fact that roads are becoming, dare I say, interesting. The Romans knew it centuries ago.

We all accept that the age of steam trains was romantic. I've got nothing against trains, in fact some of my best friends are train spotters. However I can't help feeling rail has had its day along with air travel which has become so tedious.

Now I can hear you all saying "but traffic jams are tedious too", but so long as the roads are built with the environment in mind, with plenty of trees on their fringes, built with graceful bridges, built to blend in with their surroundings, with careful thought about the needs of the cyclists, and with loads of lovely roundabouts to satisfy the British yearning for fine floral arrangements etc, then there is no need for them to be boring.

Some may sneer but roads are here to stay whether we like them or not, so let's make the most of them, we can't live without them so why not make them as aesthetically pleasing as possible. Power to the roads! Power to the roundabouts!

A delightful Droitwich "double ringer", at its centre core are flower tubs. Droitwich Brine Baths are situated in the background.

Shot at considerable risk to myself, balanced on garden railings.

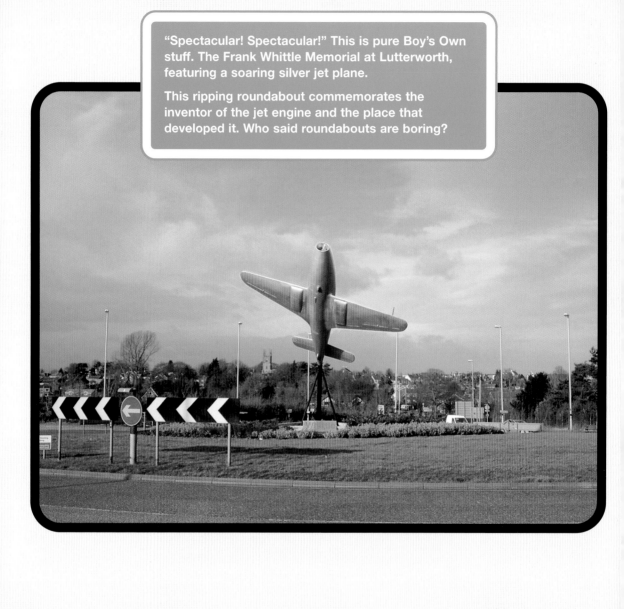

"Spectacular! Spectacular!" This is pure Boy's Own stuff. The Frank Whittle Memorial at Lutterworth, featuring a soaring silver jet plane.

This ripping roundabout commemorates the inventor of the jet engine and the place that developed it. Who said roundabouts are boring?

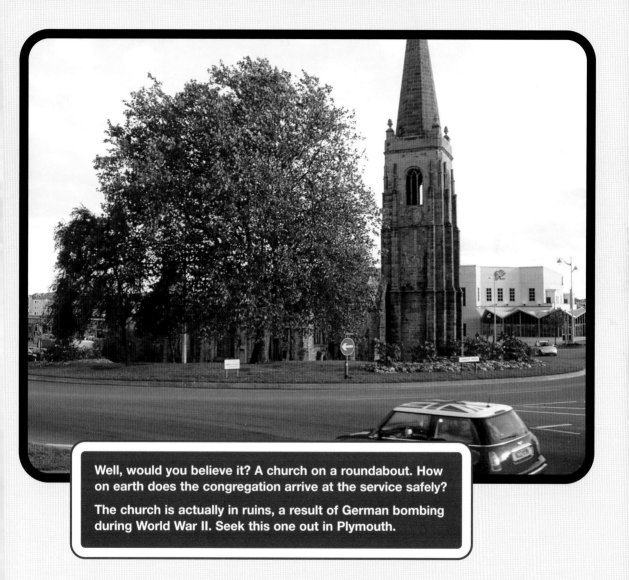

Well, would you believe it? A church on a roundabout. How on earth does the congregation arrive at the service safely?

The church is actually in ruins, a result of German bombing during World War II. Seek this one out in Plymouth.

Little cracked dome "brickie" 'bout adorned with a worn-out bollard.

Located just a short converted penalty kick from Murrayfield rugby ground.

These sliding silver characters really brighten up this bracing Blackpool 'bout.

Sideshow Bob seems to be the last one coming down. Or should that be Slideshow Bob.

Tamar Bridge traffic-island. A fine arrangement of trees, bushes, flowers and a few stray traffic cones.

Bright, bold and brassy. Blackpool merry-go-round roundabout.

You would only find something like this in Blackpool, home of hi-tack.

A Canary Wharf "chevy".

On closer inspection of this island you can just make out a "traffic light tree". The 'bout also boasts a stunning city-scape backdrop.

Why go to the Caribbean? A simply wonderful "Crusoe" island set inside Bristol town centre. This lush green paradise of an island looks good enough to have a picnic on. Which is what those guys appear to be doing. Who can blame them?

WOULD YOU BELIEVE IT, THE THINGS YOU FIND ON ROUNDABOUTS!

A pub – called "The Bowling Green", Lichfield.

Another pub plus 17 houses – "The Shepherd & Flock", Farnham, Surrey.

A church – albeit in ruins, Plymouth town centre.

A model railway – Darlington town centre.

A pagoda – Birmingham city centre.

A traffic light tree – Canary Wharf, London.

A fishing boat – Grimsby, obviously.

A boat plus a beach – Falkirk, Scotland.

A Christmas tree (Christmas time only) – Mount Hooly, Aberdeen, Scotland.

A beam engine – Aston Expressway.

An abandoned car – Skelmersdale.

Anchor chains – Birkenhead.

Milling machines – St. Helens.

Policemen in hiding – amongst the bushes on Croby Road roundabout, Leicester. (You never heard that from me alright?)

A canal lock gate – Aston again.

A replica of Stonehenge – Caenarfon

A stainless steel thingy – Elephant & Castle, London.

Two roaring lions – Sandwell, Black Country.

Spitfire fighter planes – Birmingham.

A silver jet plane – Lutterworth.

A merry-go-round – Blackpool.

A helter-skelter – also Blackpool.

A house of ill-repute – I need to check this one out.

Supermarket trolley – Skelmersdale.

Mineshaft wheel – Ironbridge.

Concrete seagulls – Morecambe.

A swimming baths – Lancaster.

Laser beam and light show – Haverhill.

Race horses – Doncaster.

Ancient settlement – Newark.

A deceased councillor's chair – Bootle.

A big brass miner's lamp – Sunderland.

A monk – Abingdon, Oxfordshire.

This blissful 'bout has a certain fairy tale feel to it.

A perfect grass circle with a perfect little pear tree. Located in a perfectly peaceful setting, Bristol Crematorium.

A grim looking P.M.T. lurking in the district of Wincolmlee. The industrial side of Hull.

WINCOLMLEE

A blinding little Bristol "brickie" sporting a white halo.

One of my all time favourites. I don't know why I love this little brick double ringer blighter so much. It has a certain gritty Northern toughness to it but it also oozes vulnerability, what with its poor battered bollard.

I have this picture up on my study wall at home and I've been known to gaze upon it for hours. Great therapy. Anyway, if you want to look it up you will find it in Hull.

Town Centre West roundabout located in Cumbernauld.

The island is made up of well cared for lawn and flower baskets devoid of flowers encompassed by red brickwork.

Lush, green Cofton Hacket island observed from a slight incline on the base of the Lickey Hills, a local beauty spot in Warwickshire.

A reverse angle shot of the Canary Wharf "traffic light tree" 'bout. (As shown on page 42.)

This picture does not boast the mighty metropolis backdrop but it does reveal more of this curious street sculpture.

One of the "Famous Five" satellite P.M.T's that make up Swindon's Magic Roundabout. (The white knuckle ride of all roundabouts.)

The mother 'bout can be seen in the distance with its tall lamppost. The hypnotic bullseye circles are typical of all Swindon's P.M.T's.

Crystal Palace mini "brickie" roundabout, in need of a bit of weeding.

On closer inspection you can make out the base of the famous Crystal Palace mast.

IT COULD HAVE BEEN US!

It's widely accepted that William Phelps Eno was the bright spark who first devised the idea of a one-way rotary system in 1903, for Columbus Circle, New York City, USA. Closely followed by Eugene Henard, Chief Architect of Paris, France in 1907. Great Britain's claim to fame in gyratory circles was that the term "roundabout" was coined by us in 1926, and replaced the term "gyratory". Our first true "gyratory flow" system was developed at Sollershott Circus, Letchworth Garden City in the late twenties. But it could have been so different, as Dr Gray of Tewkesbury has confided to me in a remarkable letter:

Dear Mr Beresford,
I have enjoyed my Christmas present [Roundabouts of Great Britain, published 2004] which has fanned the small flame which has been flickering inside me since I was a small boy. I now realise that from the age of ten I must have been a dormant roundabout spotter, but with a genetic predisposition. You see it was then that my grandmother told me in a hushed voice that her father (my great grandfather) was one of the first people in this country to promote the idea of "gyratory traffic regulation". He – Walter Noble Twelvetrees – was an eminent engineer and on 3 October 1907 gave his Presidential Address to the Civil & Mechanical Engineers Society on London Street Traffic Regulation. He did not claim to be the first to propose gyratory systems in this country, apparently a Mr. Holroyd Smith had put the idea before the London County Council ten years earlier but nothing was done. I have a copy of his address in the form of a pamphlet. It is pretty heavy-going with extremely detailed plans for gyratory systems at 11 major junctions in London. It would only be of interest to an advanced roundabout scholar but I am proud to be associated with the birth of roundabouts as we now know them.

Keep up the valuable work!

Yours sincerely,
Dr Brian Gray.

Wow, ten years before that memorable meeting when Mr Smith tabled that first proposal works out at 1807. What a shame, with more foresight and commitment Britain could have been the first country in the world to have installed a roundabout.

Pipe island, St. Helens.

Neat little "toker" ringed by light coloured brickwork.

Special thanks to Colin Beresford (no relation) for this shot.

A Manchester Airport P.M.T.

Word of warning! Be very careful if taking photographs of airport roundabouts in certain foreign countries.

Authorities abroad may not have heard of or understand the concept of roundabout spotting or why we take pictures of airport roundabouts. You could end up in detention. When those British Plane Spotters were arrested in Greece, the Greek court authorities could not get their heads round the fact that there are people out there whose actual hobby is photographing planes. What might have happened if they were Roundabout Spotters? Mind you, it's been my experience with British Bobbies that even they get suspicious when you wander outside an airport snapping roundabouts.

Sometimes I can't understand how our harmless hobby can cause so much hostility.

A real "chocolate box cover" of a roundabout. Its composition of lawn, trees and rockery makes for a perfect English 'bout if ever there was one. You can almost hear the crack of leather on willow.

I somehow get the feeling that the renowned artist Constable would have loved to have painted some of England's green and pleasant traffic islands. In saying that, this scene is not from his old stomping grounds of Suffolk, but depicts Wiltshire.

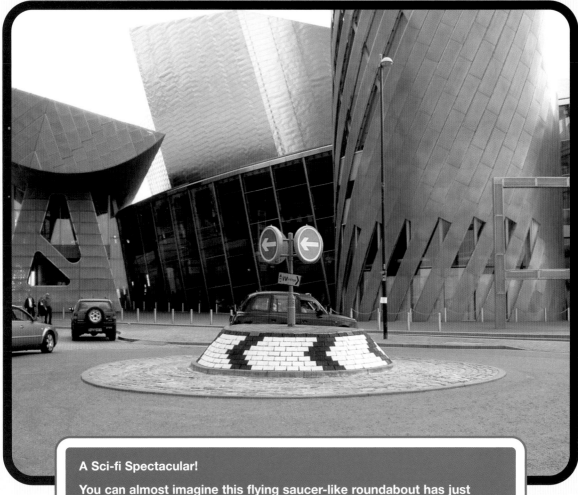

A Sci-fi Spectacular!

You can almost imagine this flying saucer-like roundabout has just landed from some far-off galaxy and its occupants have strolled into the Lowry Gallery to check out Planet Manchester's most famous artist.

Then afterwards, pondering on what a coincidence, Earthlings are made up of matchstick men and women, just like themselves.

A Shrewsbury Special.

On its central core are numerous robust plant tubs sitting on a bed of Cotswold honey coloured gravel, four direction bollards are then thrown in and garnished by a ring of green foliage before being encircled by grey granite gravel from Edinburgh. Mouth watering!

One of the most unique "chevies" I have ever seen. A cracking combination of brick and metal work, forming a mystical looking spire that seems to incorporate four fireplaces in its design.

Livingston seems to excel at this sort of thing. Great 'bout.

Elegant "double ringer" from East Anglia.
Simple and sublime symmetry.

CRAZY ABOUT THE 'BOUTS

A rather nice plus factor of being the author of *Roundabouts of Great Britain* is reading the pleasant reviews I've received. This one example, taken from the Tangents website "The Home Of Un-Popular Culture" by Dr. Marino Guida, sums up perfectly the mood and feeling of my work.

The uniqueness of "Roundabouts of Great Britain" is of course in capturing a snapshot of daily life, showing how urban design is nothing without a context to frame it in... The Sollershot Circus roundabout stands as a reminder of the things we take for granted when driving, cycling or absent-mindedly ruminating our way through town spaces. A roundabout is an oasis of calm around which parade the sights, and unsightly trail, of eager drivers making their way with varying degrees of respect for the Highway Code.

I couldn't have put it better myself. The flip-side of all this though are the accusations of me being the saddest nerd on the planet. In the previous roundabouts book I featured a Telford roundabout with a marvellous metal sculpture on it entitled "Serendipity" by the talented artist Richard Farrington. I implied that because the art was placed on a roundabout in a Telford retail park it might not be worth as much as it would if it been in the Tate Modern. Richard has since been in contact with this message:

Not sure about your comment that implies my sculpture is not worth "thousands of pounds", as I seem to remember that it actually cost £30,000 and was commissioned by a group of people that included J. Sainsbury Plc at its core.

Oooops, sorry mate. As a peace offering I'd like to mention Richard's website www.richardfarrington.co.uk which features loads more of his work.

It's also worth noting that the British Library has deposited four of my Welsh Roundabout Calendar series – Brilliant Barry Islands, Roundabouts of Cardiff, Roundabouts of Newport and Roundabouts of Swansea in their vault for future generations to ponder.

I wonder what those people will make of our fascination for roundabouts. Will we be remembered as heroes or nerds?

This riveting "red ringer" from Bracknell has a somewhat lop-sided look to it and may need some weeds pulling, but it still oozes class.

My assistant Liz Austin had to climb a tall tree (well she is younger than me) to capture this irresistible Ilfracombe P.M.T. To view it yourself you will find it close to the harbour.

A "toker" from Tyneside with four handsome bollards standing sentry and a short lamppost stuck in the middle of it.

A rugged little "brickie" caught outside Cardiff's Millennium Stadium.

The three directional signs have their own little lights attached.

Another Manchester mission from Mars U.F.O roundabout.

I don't like to spread any paranoia but they seem to gaining a foothold up north. Somebody other than me (they already think I'm barmy) should notify the authorities.

You have all been warned!

A bush and bollard combination. To the extreme right of the 'bout a stray bush appears to have broken away from the pack.

Seek this one out in Edinburgh.

Bush and brick 'bout from Brum. Rather shapeless trim to the bushes.

The picture was taken from the National Indoor Arena Car Park level three.

UNSUNG HEROES

"Never before in the field of human road engineering, has so much been owed by so many, to so few." Ernie Hill (Chairman, U.K.R.A.S.)

Who are these people who have planned, designed, built, planted, groomed and cared for our British islands? Rain or shine, sleet or snow, they have always been there for us, protecting a slice of British life. Who repairs the damage of vandals? Who plants the flowers? Who cuts the grass? Who paints the P.M.T.'s? They are the unsung heroes – The Roundabouters.

Let us now stand up and applaud this fine body of people who rarely receive any accolade for their inspired achievements. I know there is the Britain In Bloom award, but that's too broad. It's now time for a specific prize awarded to Britain's best roundabouter.

I have heard of one roundabouter who really *is* made of the right stuff. His name is Barry Crown, he's British and he is in demand all over the world as a roundabout trouble shooter. He's the Red Adair of the roundabout world.

A good example of his exploits was the case of the Clearwater roundabout in Florida, USA. Mr. Crown flew over to Clearwater to sort out an appalling mess of a roundabout, Clearwater's infamous beach roundabout. Elegant and beautiful, but a real femme fatale, capable of reducing the strongest male drivers to tears. The locals hated her that much they stopped going to the beach. Barry Crown got to work. With a bit of design tinkering he converted a roundabout with a very poor safety record INTO ONE WITH THE SAFEST. The reduction in crashes was a staggering 99.6%.

An interesting footnote coming out of the States is that crooks hate roundabouts. When being chased by the police they can always shoot a red light but can't drive around a roundabout at any great speed. Good to know.

This delightful 'bout in Bath commemorates the city's historical links with the Netherlands. The shot was taken from the second floor of Brown's restaurant, where the Author enjoyed a fish pie and lashings of ginger beer.

Very tidy Midland "chevy" with fine cut lawn, directional signs and trees.

That surely must be a swordfish under wraps. Can anyone guess where this roundabout lives?

"The Three Bears" roundabout spotted in East Kilbride.

For some reason Goldilocks wasn't part of this particular story.

A cold and frosty concrete Cumbernauld "chevy".

ARE ROUNDABOUTS SAFE FOR CYCLISTS?

Numerous people have suggested that roundabouts may well be beautiful but they can be quite dangerous for the poor cyclist. They may have a point, especially on the larger 'bouts. However, York County Council may well have come up with the answer with the Heworth Green roundabout, York's own Magic Roundabout.

The Heworth 'bout was created to ensure a safe route for the many cyclists who use the junction each day. A roundabout design was developed that incorporated annular cycle lanes. When this has been tried in the UK before, cycle lanes have always been set tight against the kerb on the outside of the island. This position means that the cyclists are almost out of sight to the driver and also makes it difficult for the cyclists to enter and exit the roundabout safely.

York's roundabout design has moved the cycle lanes closer to the centre of the roundabout which puts cyclists directly in the sight of the drivers. They've also split the lanes at each exit so it is obvious whether a cyclist is continuing around the roundabout, or if they are exiting. The roundabout also features the so called "continental design" which uses geometry to encourage lower vehicle speeds.

Indeed, average entry speeds have been brought down to 17 mph, compared with around 30 mph before. In the first year and a half of its use only one small accident was recorded and all queueing has been reduced.

Apart from being extremely functional the roundabout is also aesthetically pleasing. So come on all you roundabout designers around Britain, York has shown us the way. Cycle friendly 'bouts are possible to build. So let's have more of them!

Source: York County Council web site.

A concrete "double ringer" captured from above on a railway bridge in Carlisle.

The residue salt on the road has discoloured this 'bout so on closer inspection this "double ringer" is in actual fact a "double red ringer".

A strange Bracknell "brickie" 'bout cut into four quarters and ringed with bricks.

Another Livingston lovely.

This Newpark Roundabout has a new age feel to it. Ancient looking brickwork with inlaid veneers of copper. Quite unique!

The Miss World of Roundabouts.

Just what you would expect from the well-heeled suburb of Solihull, a town that prides itself on its well turned out roundabouts.

Immaculate display of pampas grass, flowers and shrubs with clever coloured chevron brickwork. Top drawer!

A lively Livingston mini "brickie".

On closer inspection the reader can make out snow on the peaks in the distance.

A scholarly Dulwich College 'bout in London. Quite unique with its ring of white posts and chains.

A striking Scottish chevy viewed from the M74 on a cold and frosty morning.

A Bristol "brickie-double ringer" with four round directional signs attached to its own lamppost. Spotted in the town centre.

Lizzie Brice's roundabout.

Look closely and you can make out a pointed brick sculpture.

"MAGIC ROUNDABOUTS". ARE THEY REALLY MAGIC?

Are "Magic Roundabouts" really magic? No! I don't subscribe to all this magical ring business, Lord of The Rings, Crop Circles, Stone Circles, Magic Circles. Harry Potter has a lot to answer for.

There is a school of thought that those perfect, pristine rings that appear out of nowhere during the night in our British cornfields come from alien flying saucers, attracted by our numerous roundabouts... Utter tosh! If that was the case why is it most UFO sightings occur in America where roundabouts are quite scarce?

Magic roundabouts do exist in Britain however, but do not hold any mystical powers. Not to my knowledge anyhow. They do strangely captivate me though.

My favourite maelstrom of motordom is Swindon's Magic Roundabout in Wiltshire. This is made up of one large "mother" 'bout at the centre and five small satellite P.M.T.'s in orbit around her, so to speak.

Traffic circulates in both directions. She's the white knuckle ride of roundabouts... wicked!

Similar magic roundabouts can be sighted in:
Hemel Hempstead in Hertfordshire
High Wycombe in Buckinghamshire
Denham also in Buckinghamshire
Colchester in Essex
Tamworth in Staffordshire

There is absolutely no need to fear these spectacular feats of road engineering. I know a lot of people do fear them, especially Americans, mind you they're even scared of normal 'bouts. Maybe it is just the fear of the unknown.

Take them for what they are – Magical Mystery Tours.

Pretty little "toker" from Teesside.

A roundabout combining bush, trees and grass spotted from the top of a Hereford hillside in mid-February.

Strange grass gyratory with a small bush stuck in the middle of it.

Discovered standing picket outside the Land Rover Car Plant.

At first glance this Plymouth Hoe P.M.T. looks quite normal. However on closer inspection you will notice a steel rim running around its perimeter. Quite an exciting and unique discovery. It just goes to show you can never take anything for granted when roundabout spotting.

Just two of the many bronzed gardeners that take care of this Scottish island.

Although observed from the top level of the Olympia Shopping Centre, the picture just doesn't do the scene justice. This elongated roundabout is simply littered with these strange statues all grafting away with their gardening tools...magical!

A well maintained Nottingham 'bout featuring a tidy lawn with pleasant flower and tree arrangement encircled by fine brickwork.

Good to see the "Think Bike" warnings. Roundabouts can be a bit scary for cyclists.

Brilliant "brickie" from the Black Country.

Perhaps if I may be a trifle pedantic it might be lacking a bollard for balance.

G.W.R. (God's Wonderful Roundabout). Splendid traffic island from sunny Devon.

IF THE TOWN IS RELUCTANT TO YIELD ITS ROUNDABOUTS

Sometimes you have to accept certain towns just don't have many roundabouts or their islands may be hard to locate. A reasonable quota for a day's spotting is twelve. This figure is based on experience, you have to be on a guard for burn out, many a green over eager-beaver spotter has come to grief trying too many 'bouts in one day. Remember our hobby is not a race but a journey. An island hopping journey to savour, observe, record and collect data.

Train Spotters have the advantage that their hobby comes to them; they just wait for the train to arrive. But when it does they don't go chasing after it when it leaves.

We roundabouters have to seek out our little beauties, but we do it at a leisurely pace; on foot, on a bike, or in a car it doesn't really matter so long as it is done in a serene manner. Here then lies the essence of our hobby, the seeking out of the green circles, the hunt for the Magic Rings. Not the thrill of the chase, more like a quest for the gyratory Grail.

A few tips:

Airports: Guaranteed 100% gyratory success.

Ask the locals: Don't be shy, most people love to talk about their favourite islands.

Buy a street map: It can save a lot of leg work, but I must admit it takes the fun out of the hobby. The unexpected is far more exciting.

Choose New Towns: Town planners always find room for roundabouts when presented with a blank canvas. Each new town will try to outdo their rivals with prestigious roundabout projects.

Crematoriums: They never fail, for some reason they always build a 'bout in those places. Always show respect and proceed quietly.

Seek out a supermarket retail park: You mainly find P.M.T.s, but what the hell they all count.

A wild Wilderness Roundabout crammed with red shrubs and Fir trees.

A barometer 'bout.

Built for Thames Water by Charles Henshaw & Sons Ltd, Edinburgh for the benefit of passing motorists so they can be made aware of a falling or rising barometric pressure and as such, whether good or poor weather is to be expected.

Bark seems to be in vogue on roundabouts at the moment.

Another photo taken from halfway up a tree. I actually lost a button off my cardigan to achieve this shot.

Marvellous elevated shot of a tidy looking Coventry Business Park roundabout.

The picture was taken with kind permission from the first floor of Mission Foods, a Mexican food factory.

Green and pleasant 'bout with a simple but nice arrangement of grass and a few trees.

Bathed in watery winter twilight sunshine.

Brilliant Bath beauty in full bloom.

On its inner core spring flowers have been planted and they are ringed by grass, trees, bricks and bollards. The island is complemented by one of Bath's many lovely churches in the background.

A West Midlands P.M.T. with a hexagonal drain set just off its centre.

Viewed from Redditch town centre multi-storey car park. Level ten.

"Double ringer" P.M.T. spotted from the M5 Motorway, minutes after my car had broken down during a fierce hailstorm. A good roundabout spotter is never without their camera.

Scintillating Scottish mix of kerbstone, gravel, boulder, shrub and bush, make up this superb 'bout.

VANESSA FELTZ'S BUMPS

One of the reasons why the hobby of roundabout spotting is really taking off is the fact that British town planners now seem to be coming up with more and more imaginative roundabout designs, making our pastime even more fascinating. Not content with just lawn, trees and bushes they are far more likely to emulate the continental look with sculptures, follies, oddities, statues, monuments and fountains etc.

Whilst appearing on the Vanessa Feltz BBC Radio London Show, Vanessa suggested my next project should be speed bumps...yes, speed bumps. Surely Vanessa is missing the point, speed bumps are just plain boring whereas roundabout design knows no boundaries. With so many talented artists and designers the sky really is the limit. If Andy Warhol was around today, I'm sure he would have a field day. What with giant miners lamps and merry-go-rounds appearing on our 'bouts I'm positive we would have found room for one of his giant Campbell's soup cans. You could never find a light and laser show or a soaring jet plane on a speed bump. Wouldn't you agree Vanessa?

Critics in certain quarters state that these extravagant roundabout features are distracting for drivers... Bollards! If that was the case you could never drive through a pretty Cotswold village or an interesting historical city, unless you were wearing blinkers. What would they replace them with, boring traffic lights?

I honestly think the British motorist is sick and tired of traffic lights, with their long, irritating, tedious blinking lights. Compared with our lush, green inventive islands there is no contest. 'Bouts are brilliant! 'Bouts are cool!

The Elephant & Castle roundabout. With this breathtaking rooftop aerial view we can see that it is surprisingly square shaped.
The stainless steel structure commemorates the physicist Michael Faraday, who was known for his research into electricity.

This whole scene could be a thing of the past with a multi-billion pound project planned to radically change the Elephant. Let's pray they leave the 'bouts.

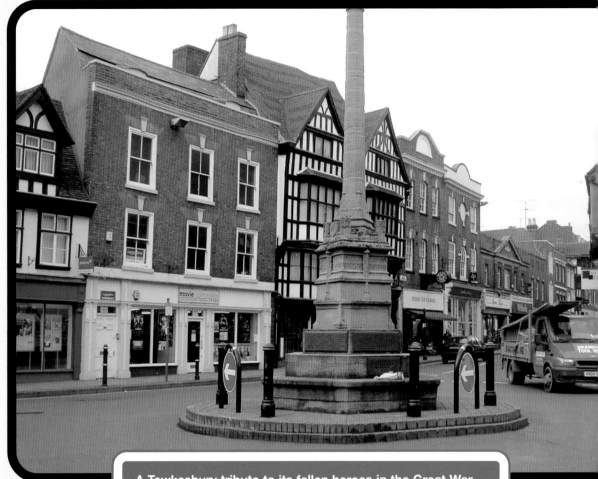

A Tewkesbury tribute to its fallen heroes in the Great War. A poignant reminder of how a roundabout can double as a functional gyratory and also serve as a war memorial.

Another First World War roundabout memorial can be found on the junction of Fosseway and the A45.

A lovely landscaped Sterling roundabout enjoying a brief sunny interlude during a chilly month of March.

The sign says it all. A Scottish multiplex "brickie" roundabout captured on a nearby bridge.

MULTIPLEX ROUNDABOUT

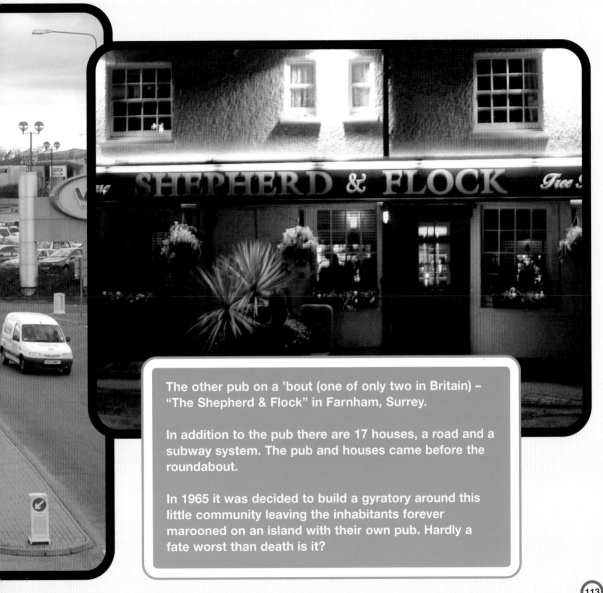

The other pub on a 'bout (one of only two in Britain) – "The Shepherd & Flock" in Farnham, Surrey.

In addition to the pub there are 17 houses, a road and a subway system. The pub and houses came before the roundabout.

In 1965 it was decided to build a gyratory around this little community leaving the inhabitants forever marooned on an island with their own pub. Hardly a fate worst than death is it?

This really is a one off. The only toll road P.M.T. found in Britain. Discovered, would you believe, in Dulwich, London, of all places.

A crushed and broken 'bout after a Friday night in Redditch.
This Phoenix will rise from the ashes, its done it before and will do it again.

UNACCEPTABLE BEHAVIOUR ON ROUNDABOUTS THAT U.K.R.A.S. CANNOT CONDONE

1. Participating in barbecues on some of the larger roundabouts.

2. Pitching your tent or caravan.

3. The Mile Round Club, A.K.A. Bonking Bouters. This trend started off with swingers in the Black Country on the park-like roundabouts common to the area.

4. The dumping of old mattresses on islands, that doesn't impress anyone.

5. Getting married on a roundabout dressed as Elvis. That is soooo tacky.

6. Picking council flowers, don't be so tight.

7. Students cramming as many of themselves as possible on a P.M.T. Even if it is for charity.

8. Driving over a P.M.T. They should be observed and navigated accordingly. Treat them with respect.

10. Councils erecting so called "street furniture" on our beloved roundabouts, i.e. sponsorship placards that are far too big for their purpose. Case in point, the ancient plot at Cross Green roundabout, Formby. The Sefton Council hopes to place one-metre billboard signs on one of Formby's most historic sites. Sacrilege! Surely small discreet billboards would suffice.

NOTE: I hate to admit this but I do feel ever so slightly guilty and hypocritical. I do recall having one divine decadent roundabout moment, taking tea and biscuits with the BBC programme "Inside Out". We were sitting on deck chairs in the middle of Britain's first roundabout, Sollershott Circus, Letchworth Garden City (the Mecca for roundabout spotters), on a lovely autumnal morning. It was utter bliss, but don't tell the committee.

Brick, grass and tree combination gyratory from Gloucester.
Located in the town centre.

The Big Blue H, Techno Park roundabout, Hamilton.
The purple heather gives this 'bout a real Scottish flavour.

A bleak out-of-season seaside scene. This Barry Island roundabout in South Wales consists of brown brick with three painted directional arrows. The out of commission public conveniences seems more like an inconvenience.

Someone seems to have taken a "slice of the cake" out of this Letchworth gyratory.

A sad South Wales traffic island very much in need of some T.L.C. Just because its location is outside Newport's semi-conductor plant, does not mean it should be so neglected.

A little "bitumen babe" discovered in Coventry city centre. Adorned with a lovely chevron skirt and three directional signs.

A sneaky shot of The College roundabout featuring nicely laid out gardens and five curious tall cones with weather vanes spinning from their tops. To view for your self, drive to the summit of the local Livingston multi-storey car park, it's free.

WHAT NEXT?

Although I've collected a large amount of roundabouts over the past years there are still areas of Britain that as yet I have not been able to reach for one reason or another. I would like for instance to explore some of the larger islands that scatter our nation. Islands for instance like the enormous "Town Centre West" roundabout in Basingstoke. Because of the 'bouts size a poor unfortunate Basingstoker died in the middle of it and wasn't discovered for four days. Rumour has it on the same very island another poor unfortunate Basingstoker went missing for several hours roaming this eerie 'bout, later claiming he was abducted by aliens. (It could only happen on a roundabout.)

Basingstoke is actually nicknamed "Doughnut City" and its roundabouts were mention in *The Hitchhikers Guide To the Galaxy*. Places like Basingstoke, Colchester, Northern Island and the South East coast line are all next on my hit list.

It's not just Tony Blair that hankers after Europe; I also feel Europe beckoning. The continentals really know how to put a 'bout together. France has far more islands than Britain and the French and Spanish are far more elaborate with their designs than we are.

America also calls. Every time I check the USA websites, more and more roundabouts are being constructed, much to the bemusement of the locals. The roundabouts are coming home, back to their roots, full circle so to speak.

And after America, why the rest of the world. (Apart from Greece of course.)

A beautiful "bitumen babe" from Hamilton. Her sensuous high-curved, yellow striped kerbs perfectly match the headdress of daffs. It's astounding that male drivers can keep their concentration with this sexy little minx roaming the streets.

ACKNOWLEDGEMENTS

Once more, special thanks must go to my assistant Liz Austin whose love for roundabouts more than matches my own. Thanks to my brother Roy Beresford for his help on the tricky London shoot. Carl Pitt should also be mentioned for riding shotgun with me around the certain rougher sides of towns and keeping news hacks in check. Heaps of praise must go to Roy Hughes who works for Reddi-Light, a Redditch based company which light up most of Britain's roundabouts. His knowledge of weird 'bouts and their whereabouts proved invaluable. Thanks also to Vince, the landlord of "The Bramley Cottage" public house, for allowing our society to use his premises, leaving him wide open to ridicule.

The UK Roundabout Appreciation Society is a group of dedicated like-minded people who meet on a regular basis to swap photographs, stories and data on all types of roundabouts. They allow anybody into their circle regardless of age, creed, colour or sex; nerds need not apply.

The UK Roundabout Appreciation Society can be contacted via the website: www.roundaboutsofbritain.com or by email: Kevin@beresfordb96.freeserve.co.uk

U.K.R.A.S. MEMBERS

Lord of the Rings:
Kevin Beresford

Ring Master:
Ernie Hill

Knights of the Inner Ring:
Roy Beresford
Richard Coffin

Ray Davies
Clive Galimore
Roy Hughes
Phill McInerny
Carl Pitt
Roger Spence

Damsels of the Inner Ring:
Liz Austin
Jo Carter
Sally Green
Sue Clark
Joan Pratten

Knights/Damsels of the Roundabout Table:
B. Bailey
Elliott Beresford
Lee Beresford
Ryan Beresford
Scott Beresford
Richard Buley
Bev Burchell

Dave Clark
Paul Clarke
Dan Fitzgerald
Deb Fitzgerald
Heather Galimore
Carol Gerrard
Norma Gray
Brian Handford
Joanne Handford
Maxwell Handford
Phil Handford
Helen Johnson
Howard Jones
Simon Mawdsley
Shirley McInerny
Pat McManus
Helen Parsons
Brian Summers
James Shwartz
Wally Tynan
Jon Williamson
Tony Wilson

Dedicated to RELATE.
For convincing my wife Linda that
roundabout spotting need not be
damaging to a relationship and
bringing us back together again.

First published in 2005 by
New Holland Publishers (UK) Ltd
London • Cape Town • Sydney • Auckland
www.newhollandpublishers.com

Garfield House, 86-88 Edgware Road
London W2 2EA
United Kingdom

80 McKenzie Street
Cape Town 8001
South Africa

14 Aquatic Drive
Frenchs Forest, NSW 2086
Australia

218 Lake Road
Northcote, Auckland
New Zealand

Copyright in text and photographs © 2005 Kevin Beresford
Copyright © 2005 New Holland Publishers (UK) Ltd

Kevin Beresford has asserted his moral right to be identified
as the author of this work.

All rights reserved. No part of this publication may be
reproduced, stored in a retrieval system, or transmitted in any
form or by any means, electronic, mechanical, photocopying,
recording or otherwise, without the prior written permission
of the publishers and copyright holders.

ISBN 1 84537 240 9

Editor: Ruth Hamilton
Designer: Paul Wright
Photographer: Kevin Beresford
Production: Hazel Kirkman
Editorial direction: Rosemary Wilkinson

10 9 8 7 6 5 4 3 2 1

Reproduction by Modern Age, Hong Kong
Printed and bound by Star Standard, Singapore